I0016508

Wordpress For Beginners:

How to Create and Set Up Your Own Website or Blog Using Wordpress

By

Joseph Joyner

Table of Contents

Introduction 5

Chapter 1. How to Setup a Website at Wordpress? 7

Chapter 2. Basic Settings 14

Chapter 3. Wordpress Plugins 22

Final Words 26

Thank You Page 27

Wordpress For Beginners: How to Create and Set Up Your Own Website or Blog Using Wordpress

By Joseph Joyner

Introduction

Wordpress is an open source platform and CMS i.e. Content Management System that was founded in year 2003 by Mike Little and Matt Mullenweg. At the initial stage, it was based on single bit of code that was made to enhance typography of day to day writing. Wordpress is the top recommended platform for all kind of blogging sites. With time, Wordpress has managed to accumulate immense appreciation by users and today's it used by millions of users. It is also one of the easiest platforms to use. Everything in it is prebaked, and by downloading the plug-in, you can make anything possible in Wordpress.

Wordpress community work day and night to create new plugins that are extremely resourceful for the bloggers in their day to day blogging. Best part of using WP is that it is free of cost and you don't have to buy any license to create a website at Wordpress. Many commercial sites are also made in WP and it is quite a successful platform with least troubles. Everything can be solved with the help of plug-ins that you can download from Google. All the plugins are easily available. As per a survey that was conducted in 2005, results said that 23.3% of 10 million site users were relying on WP.

Undeniably, Wordpress has got a warm welcome from all the users and it got amazing popularity in two years after initiation. Talking about some technical stuff, Operating system that is used by WP is Cross Platform. Coding of WP is completely done in PHP and HTML. It is basically a Blogging Software i.e., it is best suitable for blogging purposes. Wordpress Company uses GNU GPL v2+ license.

To sum up the introduction part, I would say that Wordpress is an ultimate platform to create blogging site. You can find free themes, plugins and there are thousands of other features that make WP worth using for your website. Let me know take you to step 2, take a look below:

Chapter 1. How to Setup a Website at Wordpress?

As far I have observed, I would recommend my readers that best way to create a website is to start with its blog. There are many platforms that help you in creating free blogging sites. Among all other platforms, Wordpress is most recommended platform and first choice of millions of bloggers.

For a fact, many people think that creating a website is a tricky task and it requires a lot of skill, money and time. Well, I would say that creating a website is the easiest task only if you know the right platform and hosting service.

Best part of creating an account at Wordpress is that it is least complicated and with the help of tutorials and articles that are easily available at Google, you can setup a website. You don't need any technical help in case of these platforms. I will explain the process in detail that will help you in easy setup of website in WP.

1: Firstly, it is essential to muster up all your resources. Among the requisites of resources, you need

Domain Name: Domain name is the prime requirement of any website. It is the unique identity of a website that will be the title of your online business.

Payment Mode: As we are undertaking every process via internet, the only payment mode that can help you in making payment is a credit card or a debit card. By filling the details of your card, you can purchase hosting and make other essential payments (where required).

Time: Patience is important. Although it is not a long process, still you need to keep calm and follow step by step approach to setup the site.

2: Next step is to **Set up a Hosting Account**. There are many web hosts available online that offers most fantastic services at extremely economical prices. There are some parameters that need to be considered while selecting a web hosting site for your website. Take a look at the factor below:

Customer Support: Customer support of every hosting website is the prime factor that must be considered. These days, accessing the creditability is quite simple as you can check out the reviews about the site and see what other people have to say about it. Web host must offer 24-7 customer support via email, call or live chat.

Easily Usable: Web Hosts that offer easily usable services are considered as best hosts. The services must be understandable so that a non-familiar person can also access the services.

Reliability: Reliability is another important factor that must be considered. If your web host is not reliable then you will have to live in a threat as long as your site is associated with that host. In reliability factor, you must considered uptime of at least 99.9%.

Unlimited Disk Space and Band Width: Whether you have a small website or large, every user needs unlimited disk space and Bandwidth. Always keep an eye open for both these essentials before settling on at a web hosting company.

Affordable Packages: Hosing companies offer great deals in packages so, you must select the company that offers all the required services in minimum prices.

Therefore, after selecting an accurate hosting service and setting up an account, register for domain name.

You can register domain name at any of the hosting websites that offer this particular service. You just have to fill the name that you like and select the extension for example: .com, .net, .org, .biz, etc. Then click next button to move to next step. As you have to purchase domain name, you must put in your card credentials and purchase it. Pick the package that suits your budget and finally you can click at complete button. A page will display where you have to create a password. Type the password of your choice but make sure that it is complex enough so that no one can hack your account. You can then use that password wherever required.

As a result, your account will be created and you can finally login to your domain. Although, domain name is prefilled in the field but in any case it is not, you can fill the credentials and login to your domain. You will then witness number of pop ups that will come up with many new options. You don't have to focus on them and keep declining them as they appear. Simply press next button to move to next window. Home screen or usually called welcome screen will appear as you click at next button in previous screen. From there, you need to do some settings so visit cPanel.

3: It's time to **Install Wordpress** now. As the screen displays in front of you, you don't have to panic on seeing number of buttons. The installation process is extremely simple and it doesn't have anything to do with this page full of buttons. All you have to do is to move down to option called **Website Builders**. From the options displayed, simply click at the logo of Wordpress. Another window will open where you will see number of scripts. All you have to do is to click at Wordpress logo. While you click, your Mojo account will open that is basically used to manage automated scripts. After that, another window will appear that is known as Install Wordpress window. In that window, simply click at start button to initiate the process.

As you proceed, another window will appear asking you to select the domain. If you find any error then simply click at "Check Domain". It might be possible that you receive a message saying "Oops, Looks like something already exist there". Don't panic and simply select the option "Continue". Sometimes, domains have some in-built directories so all you need to do is to select the option of "Continue". This will overwrite all the existing files. Options differ with every hosting site. I am just writing these options in general. Most of hosting sites follow similar process so you just have to select the options carefully.

Now, as another screen will appear, simply click at "Check Domain". Another screen will appear saying that process is almost done. There will be certain checkboxes but select them as per your requirement. A checkbox will appear with "Advanced settings" option. Well, at this moment of time, you don't have to put yourself into it so keep it unchecked. Simply enable the options of terms and conditions and click at "Install" button. As the process takes few minutes, you need to keep calm and let the process take place calmly. After installation process is over, another window will appear that will display Blog URL, Login URL, Username and Password.

4: Time to load **New Blog**. Open a new tab and paste URL address in it and click enter. A very simple and ordinary theme will be displayed on the screen. There are thousands of themes in Wordpress that are available online. You can use them later on to beautify your blog. The default theme is quite simple and ordinary.

5: **Login** to your Account. As loading finishes and screen is displayed in front of you, you will see a form asking for Username and Password. As you fill credentials, simply click at "Login". As you login to your account, another window will appear displaying Dashboard and other options at Homepage.

6: Write your **first post**. As you have setup a website now, it's time for action. You must have waited a long time for the website to go online and you can color it with your passion of writing. It's time to add your first post. Simply go to posts and click at "Add Post". A screen will display with different fields. In the title field, add the title of your blog. In the body field, add the body of article and make the settings of the text like alignment, bold, italic, bullets, etc. In this way, Wordpress is considered as the easiest blogging platform.

So, this was all the process about setting up Wordpress website.

Chapter 2. Basic Settings

Now, next milestone is about basic settings that every blogging account requires.

Although there are a number of settings and advanced settings but you don't have to make them at initial stages. As you keep on learning how to use Wordpress and exploring new things, you will be able to make advanced settings. For now, I am going to describe all the primary settings in a newly made Wordpress site. Take a look below:

1: Permalinks: Firstly, it is essential to know all about permalink. What is the definition of a Permalink?

Well Permalink is called the URL of the blog that you have posted on your website. It is also known as Permanent link. It is added to the database. It creates uniqueness of every blog and makes it different from one another. Most of the bloggers are not familiar with the term Permalink. It is popularly known as Permanent Link.

So, this was all about the definition of Permalink.

Wordpress Settings for Permalink

Firstly, it is recommended that default permalink must be replaced with custom permalink. Mostly, default permalink appears in following format:

http://domainname.com/p=52354

In this format, you will find the URL of the blog. Now, if anytime you find a blog with such a permalink, simply analyze that blogger has not done its permalink settings yet. This type of format is also not friendly with Search Engine rules. There was a time when bloggers use to find it quite complex to change permalink settings. With the initiation of latest version, you will find settings straight forward and least tricky. There is a process to change permalink settings. All you have to do is to go to **Settings**, a screen will appear with number of options. Go to **Permalink**. Another window will appear and you have to select the post name from the menu. After that, simply click at **save**.

Now, you will see that the URL of blog has changed with the title of blog. In this way, you will be able to do better SEO of your blog as well. Also note that, if you have not made these primary changes and have not converted default permalink to custom permalink, you can change it through **301 Redirection Process**.

So, this was the process of changing Permalink in your blog. It is quite an important setting you every blogger must take care of this one. Marketing and promotion of the blog is highly required. So, you will need it later on when you will begin with the process of Search Engine Optimization for your blog.

2: Security Changes: Security of your blog is the major concern. Given the type of hacking stunt that people use to destroy your website and hack all your confidential data, it is important to make all possible security changes on your site. In Wordpress, making security settings is quite simple and Wordpress being a renowned platform to use for blogging, you can rely on the settings. Admin security is the settings that need to be done to keep your website save. Here is the process that will help you making changes with Admin security. Google is puffed up with the articles and tutorials that are very helpful in using Wordpress. Even this article can help you learn basic security settings. You must make these settings to keep your site away from brute attack. The process might seem tricky but, trust me, it is not. Follow the steps: Firstly, you have to create a User in your account and fashion it with all the admin rights. Next step is to move to the login page and add that ID to login. While you visit in the user's page, you have to delete default admin account. This is the smartest way to stay away from default admin and making a user will help you save confidential data. For further security, I would recommend to use a tricky password for user's account. If you find it hard to remember then you can use Ctrl+ C to copy the password and make a document in word and use Ctrl+ V to paste it there. This will escape you from the trouble of remembering complex passwords. I would say it again that you must make sure that password is hard to guess and extremely complex. It will keep you from getting hacked and add more security to your account.

3: Settings to Disable User Registration: Some blogging sites allow users the provision of guest posting. This is also a very popular stunt of popularizing sites. In such a case, it is important to keep a check on keeping user registration open. Firstly, you must clear it into your mind that whether or not you want to allow guest posting on your site. There are many other settings that come all the way with guest posting. Tasks such as managing posts and allowing the ones that are worth to be posted on your website etc are important to be undertaken. Also the settings must be done accordingly. Although, opening registrations is a good thing but obviously, it will bring some drawbacks along-with. The worst part is spam registration that comes along-with. These are super headache that will agitate you a lot. Guest Blogging also very much depends upon the type of blog you have. If your blogging site does not require guest blogging then I will recommend that you must disable the settings of user registration. There is a process that you can follow to disable the settings. Firstly, you have to go to settings. From the panel of options, click at Wordpress registration. This will bring you to another page full of options. Select general in the options that are being displayed. By clicking at General, you have actually changed the settings and no user will be able to register with your site.

These were other essential yet common settings that must be done.

4: Settings of Time: Time settings are among basic setting in every website. This also helps blogger to schedule their posts. It is not necessary that bloggers are available to post the content online at every hour of the day. Sometimes, posts are scheduled at odd hours. For that, you need to schedule them so that they can go online by themselves at a specific time. Time settings help in better processing of scheduler. To make time settings, all you have to do is to follow certain steps. Simply go to settings, there you have to select the option of general settings. From there, go to change time zone. BY visiting to this options, another screen will appear and you can select the time zone of your country and make time settings manually. Also you can set default option that will keep time updated all the time. These settings will make it easy for you to schedule your post and free from the complexity of manually posting your blog at every hour of day.

5: Settings for Wordpress Threaded Comment: Wordpress blogs allow two type of commenting. According to the conventional commenting, users are allowed to post only one comment. Today's methods are different. Now, users can make threaded comments i.e. they can post any number of comments as they want. Conventional commenting supported only one comment which was called Original comment and second type of commenting is known as Threaded comment. With the help of threaded comments, users have the freedom to reply to other reader's comments as well and therefore a blog becomes a hub where like-minded people can discuss a topic. This is also a great way to keep your readers on the blog page for maximum time. Nowadays, all the blogs have become discussion boards. You need to make certain settings to allow threaded commenting on your blog. Process is given below:

Firstly go to settings and there you will find a discussion tab. A screen will display with numerous options. You don't have to get puzzled with the options. Look for a checkbox called "Threaded Comment and Break comments", you will have to enable the option and allow users to discuss your blog. This will also help you to increase retain ability of users on your blog.

6: Settings of Comment Gravatar: Gravatar allows you to add images in your comment. It is a fantastic feature. These are useful images that are only displayed on the screen of users that have signed up to your site. Mostly, it is available to those that have subscribed or signed up for your site. For all the other users that have not signed up with your site will not be able to see these images. In such a case, if you want to make these images public, you need to do certain settings. It helps in socializing your work more and fetching more readers. All you have to do is to go to settings, then click at the option of discussions and enable the option. This will show the images to all your readers. It frees the account from any kind of parameters. It is a fabulous feature and will help in getting more appreciation of users. Also, in this way, more customers are fascinated to the site and you will be able to enjoy more readers to your account.

Therefore, these are all the primary settings of a newly made Wordpress website.

Chapter 3. Wordpress Plugins

Next Milestone is of Plugins that are used in Wordpress sites. Plugins are extremely necessary or easy and convenient usage of Wordpress blogs. These are premade codes that specialize in certain kind of process. These plugins helps in easy processing of tasks in Wordpress sites. It is quite simple to download plugins. All you have to do is that while you are in dashboard screen, there is an option at left end of the screen called Plugins. Simply click at that option. A new window will appear with many new options and a search bar. You just have to fill the name of the plugin that you like to add in your account. While you press search button, plugins that are available with different companies will be displayed in front of you. Select the one that is most appreciated by users and download it. This is the simplest way to add plugin to your Wordpress Blogging account.

There are few Plugins that are must to be there in your Wordpress account. Take a look at few of them below:

1: Akismet: Akismet is an ultimate plugin that every blogger must have in his blogging account. As blogging

allow users to post their comments on the blog. There are some spam comments that can ruin the reputation of your blog. To get rid of any spam comment in your blog, you can use Akismet plugin. It will guard your account from comment spam. As I already mentioned, this is a must have plugin in your Wordpress account.

2: Backup Wordpress: Every blogger must keep backup of all his files and blogs. An awesome plugin is available in Wordpress that helps you in creating backup of your site including database and all other files. It is an automatic update of backup that keeps on protecting the data of your site time on time. You can also schedule your update as after how many days ypou want the update process to take place.

3: **SEO by Yoast**: Search Engine Optimization is extremely essential for every blogging site. You cannot avoid the process if you want your blog to rank high in Google searches. SEO is a huge set of processes that helps in promoting the blogs and making it a brand. SEO by yoast is the best and most followed plugin for all kind of SEO process to undertake in a Wordpress account. It is specially downloaded for on-page SEO. There are numerous processes that are done by this ultimate app. Given the popularity of Wordpress sites, SEO by yoast is among the mandatory plugin that must be available in every blogging site.

4: Google Analytics for Wordpress: Analytics is among SEO tools that are quite mandatory for website in every platform. With the help of Plugin named Google Analytics for Wordpress, it will help you in adding analytics to your Wordpress account.

5: Contact Form 7: Contact form is a prime option that is available in every website. Plugin called Contact Form 7 is user friendly and it helps you in managing contact options. It will help customers in managing multiple contact form at same time. Also it will help you in customizing the form and managing content. Among all other contact plugins, it is the simplest and easy plugin that is also most recommended for users of Wordpress.

6: FeedBurner FeedSmith: All the feeds of your Wordpress account must be managed and FeedBurner helps in managing all your feeds and directs them to your FeedBurner Feeds. This is the utmost way to track all your customers. Also it is the best way to stay in touch with customers.

7: Google AdSense Plugin: Google AdSense is a quick and interesting way to allow adds on your blog and make easy money. After some time, when blog manages to attain enough popularity, you will surely need this plugin for managing AdSense. With the help of this plugin, you can set parameters such as format of ads on your website. The format includes Text ads, images ads, both text and image ads, etc. Also you can manage positioning of the ads.

Final Words

So, here I sum up with the Wordpress guide. For quick revision, topics that have been covered in this book are:

1: An Introduction to Wordpress

2: How to setup a website at Wordpress

3: Primary Settings after installing Wordpress

4: Plugins to use in Wordpress

I have tried to make all the concepts clear in this book. Hope this guide will help you you're your Wordpress site. Happy Blogging!

Thank You Page

I want to personally thank you for reading my book. I hope you found information in this book useful and I would be very grateful if you could leave your honest review about this book. I certainly want to thank you in advance for doing this.

If you have the time, you can check my other books too.

www.ingramcontent.com/pod-product-compliance
Lightning Source LLC
Chambersburg PA
CBHW071554080326
40690CB00056B/2044